Weather Update

Blizzards

by Nathan Olson

Consultant:
Joseph M. Moran, PhD
Associate Director, Education Program
American Meteorological Society
Washington, D.C.

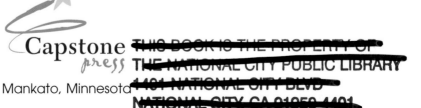

Capstone
press

Mankato, Minnesota

Bridgestone Books are published by Capstone Press,
151 Good Counsel Drive, P.O. Box 669, Mankato, Minnesota 56002.
www.capstonepress.com

Library of Congress Cataloging-in-Publication Data
Olson, Nathan.
    Blizzards / by Nathan Olson.
        p. cm.—(Bridgestone books. Weather update)
    Includes bibliographical references (p. 23) and index.
    ISBN 0-7368-4330-2 (hardcover)
    1. Blizzards—Juvenile literature. I. Title. II. Series.
QC926.37.O38 2006
551.55'5—dc22   2004029077

Summary: A brief introduction to blizzards, including how they form, where they happen, and
    blizzard safety.

Editorial Credits
Jennifer Besel, editor; Molly Nei, set designer; Kate Opseth, book designer; Wanda Winch,
    photo researcher; Scott Thoms, photo editor

Photo Credits
Art Directors/Spencer Grant, 8
Aurora/IPN/ASA/Andoni Canela, 14
Bruce Coleman Inc./Erwin & Peggy Bauer, 1
Corbis/Jim Reed, 16; Reuters, 10
Digital Vision/Daniel Pangbourne, 12
Getty Images Inc./Alvis Upitis, cover; Chris Hondros, 4; Time Life
    Pictures/Wallace G. Levison, 20
Photri MicroStock/F. Siteman, 18

Table of Contents

What Are Blizzards?

Falling snow whips through the air. On the ground, wind pushes snow into large **drifts**. Schools and businesses close. A dangerous blizzard rages outside.

Blizzards are strong winter storms. They have snow, high winds, and cold temperatures. Winds blow at least 35 miles (56 kilometers) per hour. Temperatures fall below freezing, 32 degrees Fahrenheit (0 degrees Celsius). Blowing snow makes everything outside look white.

◄ During a blizzard, blowing snow and deep drifts make walking outside difficult.

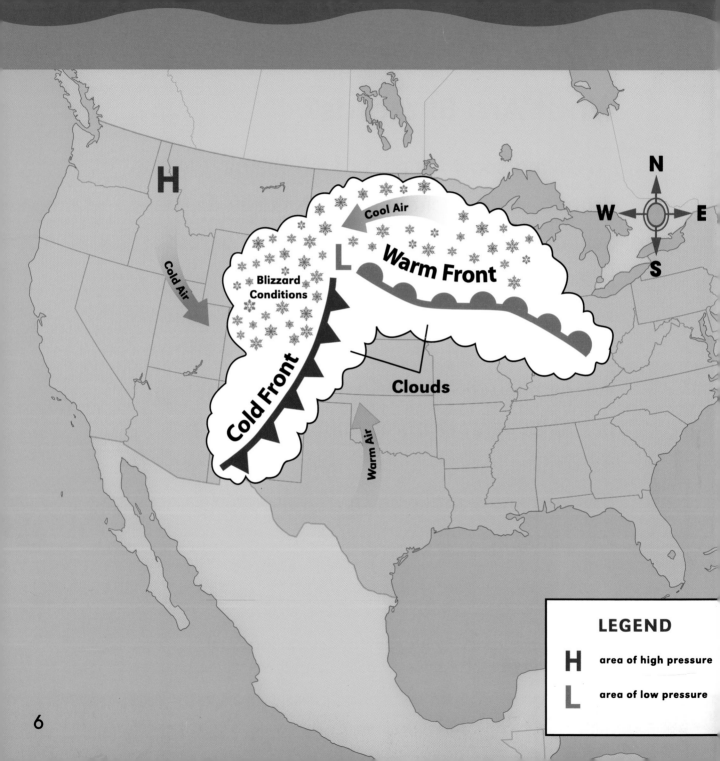

How Blizzards Form

Blizzards happen when **air masses** meet and form a **front**. Along the front, warm air rises. As it rises, the air cools and clouds form.

Snow is made by water droplets and ice **crystals** inside a cloud. Some of the water droplets **evaporate** into a gas called vapor. As the vapor freezes to the ice crystals, the crystals grow larger and begin to fall. The crystals then crash into other crystals and make snowflakes. Snowflakes combined with high winds and cold temperatures make a blizzard.

◄ Snow forms inside clouds. During a blizzard, strong winds blow falling snow through the air.

Where Blizzards Happen

Blizzards can happen anywhere, if the weather is right. For blizzards to form, temperatures need to be below freezing. Blizzards also need falling snow and wind.

In North America, blizzards happen most often in the north-central and northeastern areas. The East Coast of the United States has blizzards called nor'easters. Blizzards don't usually happen in warm places, like Arizona, because temperatures do not get cold enough.

◀ People walk down a street in Boston after a nor'easter buried their cars in snow.

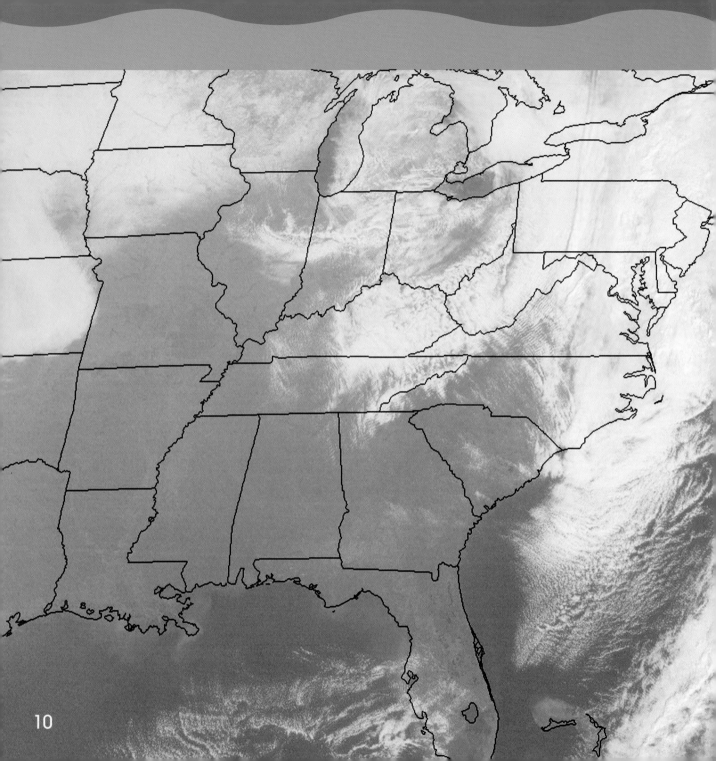

Forecasting Blizzards

Meteorologists are scientists who **forecast** the weather. They use pictures taken from space to see where snow is falling. They also keep track of air fronts, temperatures, and winds.

Meteorologists look at many things to tell when a blizzard may form. They measure how much moisture is in the air. Meteorologists can then tell how much snow might fall.

Meteorologists also study wind speeds. Winds that blow at least 35 miles (56 kilometers) per hour in a snowstorm can cause a blizzard.

◀ Scientists study pictures taken from space to tell where a blizzard might hit.

TOMORROW

Blizzard

Highs: 15-22
Winds: NW 35-45

Watches and Warnings

The National Weather Service puts out weather watches and warnings. A winter storm watch means heavy snow or ice could fall soon. A winter storm warning means unsafe winter weather has begun. Watches and warnings are announced on TV and the radio to prepare people for winter storms.

A blizzard warning is the most serious winter storm message. This warning means temperatures will become very cold. Winds will speed up.

◄ People watch TV to learn about the latest winter weather alerts.

Blizzard Dangers

Blizzards can be dangerous. Winds push snow into deep drifts. Sometimes blizzards cause a condition called a **whiteout**. In a whiteout, the snow in the air, the snow on the ground, and the clouds all look white. Whiteouts make seeing very difficult.

A blizzard's below-freezing temperatures are also dangerous. Uncovered skin can freeze, causing **frostbite**. The cold conditions can also lower people's body temperatures. This condition, called **hypothermia**, can cause illness or death.

◄ Blowing and drifting snow makes driving dangerous and difficult during a blizzard.

Blizzard Safety

People need a safety plan during blizzards. They should stay indoors and wear warm clothing. They should also have flashlights, radios, and batteries in case the electricity goes out.

Blizzards make driving unsafe. People should not drive during a blizzard. If they need to drive, people should be prepared. All cars should have emergency kits in them. These kits need to have food, water, warm clothes, a shovel, and a flashlight.

◀ A car is buried in a snow drift after sliding off the road during a blizzard.

After a Blizzard

Cleanup begins when the blizzard ends. Plows clear snow from the streets. People shovel snow from their sidewalks and steps.

After a blizzard, people should be careful when going outside. Temperatures may still be very cold. They should dress in warm clothes. If their clothes get wet, they should go back inside. Wet clothes can keep the body from staying warm.

◄ Cleaning up after a blizzard is hard work. Snow must be shoveled off sidewalks and driveways.

Major Blizzards in History

The most famous blizzard in U.S. history happened in 1888. This storm was called the "Great White Hurricane." The storm dumped 5 feet (1.5 meters) of snow in some parts of New York. At least 400 people died in the storm.

The Superstorm of 1993 hit the East Coast of the United States. At least 250 people died in this three-day nor'easter. Schools, airports, and businesses closed due to the weather.

Blizzards are powerful winter storms. Being prepared for a blizzard is the best way to stay safe.

◀ The "Great White Hurricane" buried the entrance to the Grand Opera House in New York City.

Glossary

air mass (AIR MASS)—a huge volume of air that is uniform in temperature and humidity

crystal (KRISS-tuhl)—an object with a pattern of flat surfaces

drift (DRIFT)—a pile of snow created by wind

evaporate (e-VAP-uh-rate)—to change from a liquid to a gas

forecast (FOR-kast)—to say what you think will happen to the weather

front (FRUHNT)—the place where two air masses meet

frostbite (FRAWST-bite)—an injury to the body caused by very cold temperatures

hypothermia (hye-puh-THUR-mee-uh)—a dangerous condition that happens when a person's body temperature becomes very low

whiteout (WITE-out)—a blizzard condition that makes objects hard to see

Read More

Allen, Jean. *Blizzards.* Natural Disasters. Mankato, Minn.: Capstone Press, 2002.

Chambers, Catherine. *Blizzard.* Wild Weather. Chicago: Heinemann, 2002.

Internet Sites

FactHound offers a safe, fun way to find Internet sites related to this book. All of the sites on FactHound have been researched by our staff.

Here's how:
1. Visit *www.facthound.com*
2. Type in this special code **0736843302** for age-appropriate sites. Or enter a search word related to this book for a more general search.
3. Click on the **Fetch It** button.

FactHound will fetch the best sites for you!

Index